Sing a Song of Seasons
Singing with Children Series

"Sing the new songs! Sing with Joy!
...not only with your tongue,
but with your life!..."
St. Augustine

By Mary Thienes Schunemann
Illustrations by Lura Schwarz-Smith

a naturally you can sing™ production

Sing a Song of Seasons

Parent/Teacher Resource
Songbook & CD

By Mary Thienes Schunemann

If you can walk, you can dance…
        If you can talk, you can sing!!!
                              Zimbabwe

Copyright 2008 naturally you can sing™
All Rights Reserved. No part of this book may be reproduced or transmitted in any form or by any means electronic or mechanical, including photocopying, recording, or by any information or retrieval system without written permission of publisher.

Thienes Schunemann, Mary 1960 – 2007
Sing a Song of Seasons: Singing with Children Series
ISBN 0-9708397-0-7

Fourth Edition: February 2005
Third Edition: September 2002
Second Edition: February 2001
First Edition: October 2000

Grateful acknowledgement is made for permission to print songs from colleagues and friends. Every effort has been made to trace ownership of all copyrighted material. If any omission has been made, please bring this to the attention of the publisher so that proper acknowledgment may be given in future editions.

Cover Design/Illustrations:	Copyright 2002 Lura Schwarz-Smith
Wordsmith/Layout:	Lesleigh Lippitt/Sven Schunemann
Music Production:	Jonathon Leubner, Surround in Sound Studio, Milwaukee, WI
Music Notation:	Mary Thienes Schunemann
Editor:	Helen Blake

naturally you can sing™ productions
157 Ellsworth Road, Blue Hill, Me 04614

To Order:
Tel: 415-827-8545
www.naturallyyoucansing.com
E-mail: sing@naturallyyoucansing.com

Printed and bound in Ellsworth, Maine

To earth I come to greet the light
To greet the sun
The stones which rest
The plants which grow
The beasts which run
To greet all people
Who live and walk
Who work and will
Love God in all
Then God greets me
In all I do
And I and you in God are one…
R. Steiner

This songbook is dedicated to my dear friend Mary Clare -
a lover of singing and children.

Sing a Song of Seasons
Table of Contents

Track		Page	Track		Page
	Author Notes..................	3		AUTUMN	
	On Children and Nature.....	4-5	23	September Passing By...............	29
			24	Five Golden Leaves.................	30
			25	The Leaves are Green...............	31
	SPRINGTIME		26	Scarlet and Yellow...................	32
1	I'm a Tall, Tall Tree.............	6	27	Oh, Great Spirit......................	33
2	In the Springtime.............	7	28	The Farmer...........................	34-35
3	The Heart of a Seed..........	8	29	The Winds............................	35
4	I Have Heard a Mother Bird	9	30	Jack O' Lantern.....................	36
5	Spring Rain......................	10-11	31	The Squirrel.........................	37
6	Growing Song...................	12	32	Reaping Song.......................	38-39
7	The Morning Star..............	13	33	The Apple Tree.....................	40
8	Pussy Willows...................	14	34	Autumn Goodbye..................	40
9	Caterpillar........................	15			
10	Butterflies.......................	16		WINTER	
11	Branch of Snowy May.........	17	35	Light of the Sun is Fading..........	41
12	Springtime Goodbye..........	17	36	My Little Lamp......................	42
			37	The North Wind Doth Blow.......	43
	SUMMER		38	Jack Frost............................	44
13	The Cuckoo.....................	18-19	39	Old Man Winter.....................	45
14	Over in the Meadow...........	20-21	40	Winter Song.........................	46
15	Nimble Fishes...................	21	41	I'm a Little Snowman..............	47
16	Zoom! Zoom! Zoom!..........	22	42	Mark Your Steps....................	48
17	It's Hot!	23	43	Oh Where Do You Come From?..	48
18	Day at the Beach..............	24	44	One Star Shone.....................	49
19	A Little Green Frog...........	25	45	The Buffalo in Winter...............	50-51
20	Fireflies..........................	26	46	How We Do Love the Snow........	52-53
21	Falling Stars.....................	27	47	The Groundhog.....................	54
22	Summer Goodbye.............	28	48	Winter Goodbye....................	54
				Resources...........................	55
				Loving Thanks......................	56
				Song of Dzitbalche..................	57
				Available From......................	58
				Quick & Easy Order Forms.........	59

Sing a Song of Seasons

On Young Children and Music

At this time in our culture, human beings sing less than they have in the history of the world. As we become more removed from our voices, we become removed from ourselves, each other, and that which is most human and joyful in us. Singing with our children is truly one of the greatest gifts that we can give them. When we sing from our heart, whether to accompany the task at hand, to bring our child's attention to something, or purely for the joy of sharing a song together, we awaken a deep and joyful place in our souls. These are places music can touch deeply.

The young child lives in the world of music and imagination in a very different way than the adult. Rhythm and tempo are very free for them, as is their relationship to pitch. To the young child, music and movement are one. When they hear and participate in live music, sung or played, their whole inner being is nourished and vitalized.

Recent research also indicates that a wide range of early musical experiences have a powerful effect on the preschooler and kindergartner, influencing their language development, as well as increasing concentration, memory, visual, and listening skills, spatial orientation, and physical coordination. For children, these are all important building blocks for their future learning and success in life. And it can be done in such fun and meaningful ways!

The music in this songbook reflects a variety of mood: happy; joyful; quiet and peaceful; fast and rollicking; slow and calm; high and low. This is how we can create many different kinds of moods with children that mirror both the outer world of nature and the developing inner world of the child. Though there are tempo markings and barlines in these songs, I encourage you to find your own way to sing the songs – faster in some parts, and slower in others. This will bring the songs to life and make them vibrant for you and your children.

My hope is that this songbook will help you grow more confident with our voice so that you will have courage to make up your own nature songs to sing with the children. Let them help you! Children are some of the best songwriters I know!

A friend told me that other day that she can't sing very high and felt daunted. I reassured her that songs are arranged in such a way as to mix high-pitched songs and low-pitched songs, so that her voice will be exercised in a fun and playful way.

You, too, will find that the more you explore and play with your voice, the easier singing becomes!

A Note on Instrumentation

In the written music for some of the songs you will find the music for the playful, happy sound of a children's harp, or lyre. The lyre is a simple instrument with seven strings which anyone can easily pick up and play. Because of its traditional folk scale, all the notes sound in tune and it always sounds magically beautiful. There are also some songs which are accompanied by a Native American drum!

Please refer to the Resources Page in the back of the songbook for more information.

On Children and Nature
By Cynthia Aldinger

What was it that day twenty years ago, when my young son came running into the house, eyes widened, breathless, and full of both wonder and trepidation? What had he seen? He tried to scribe it – a shadow, but not really a shadow. It moved quickly, and then it was gone. It had looked at him!

To the young child, everything has 'being-ness,' and nowhere more than in the world of nature. It is a world that can at once delight, awe, and even frighten. And children cannot get enough of it! A favorite story is one I heard from a friend in Denmark describing a toddler who spent half an hour exploring a knothole in a tree. His finger went in, it came back out, it went in again, came back out again.

Nature to the young is more than pretty flowers and beautiful sunsets and rainbows. It is a kingdom unto itself, and the child holds the scepter if given the freedom to explore. Ah, the glory of the movement of an earthworm, the worlds of the firefly, the delight of the wind playing among the leaves, the fear of the shadow, and, of course, the chance meeting of a woodland fairy!

While watching a child in a natural environment one almost feels it is the child's true home. By experiencing the daily, monthly, and seasonal rhythms of the earth and its surrounding heavens, the child learns to breathe in a way that can be experienced as having a flexibility of soul. Living deeply into the outer forms of nature can develop the life-long capacity to meet more fully the inner life of a fellow human being.

Of course, playing outside and going on nature walks are often the best vehicles for learning to overcome out own obstacles. I will never forget a young boy I taught in kindergarten many years ago who would build a 'cave' for himself out of wooden playstands and cloths every day when he arrives. He would go inside and, peeking through a crack in the cloths, watch the other children play. He was quite afraid of being social.

Across the street from our school there was a marvelous outdoor environment that the children dubbed "The Fairy Glen." It was quite rugged and required agility and perseverance o work oneself down the sloping hillsides and across huge fallen trees and large boulders. This same boy was overwhelmed every time we went for a walk to the Fairy Glen. Yet, one glorious day, I heard his little voice calling out to me, "Look!" He was standing in the middle of one of the fallen trees across a chasm that was significantly deep for a young child. He was breathing! From that day forth, he played with the other children and participated in all the activities of the kindergarten. Nature can bring such a healing force into the life of a child.

Today, in our fast-paced technology culture, time spent in nature can provide balance for the inner life of the child. A child will sometimes need the loving guidance of an adult who has remembered the joys of the natural world. In the words of Rachel

Carson: "If a child is to keep alive his inborn sense of wonder....s/he needs the companionship of a least one adult who can share it, rediscovering with them the joy, the excitement and mystery of this world we live in."

There are times when Nature asks us to be silent and observe. Coming upon a beautiful golden garden spider sitting in the center of its perfectly woven orb requires nothing more from us than an open-eyed sense of wonder. At other times, like a fresh snowfall, a rain day, or remembering one of God's special creatures, we sing and celebrate. Whether you are a teacher doing circle time with your children, a mom or dad who understands the importance of music in our child's life, or someone who likes to break out into a little ditty now and the, this collection of nature songs can be a welcome support to awaken in us the memory of our relationship to nature and its inhabitants.

Sing! Blessing on you and all the fortunate children who come into your care!

Cynthia Aldinger, founder of LifeWays North America, Teacher Trainer, Waldorf Kindergarten teacher.

How to use this Songbook & CD
- Play the CD
- Look at the music as you listen
- Enjoy the simple melodies
- Hum and sing along with me
- Then sing to the children in your life!

This series, Singing with Children, was inspired by the many adults I teach who want to gain confidence in their singing voices. The songs are easy to learn. Let the music be a roadmap to help guide you as you sing.

Remember: It is not as important how you sing, but that you sing with children!

Track 1   # I'm a Tall, Tall Tree   Traditional

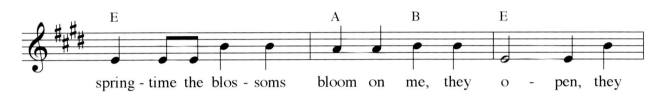
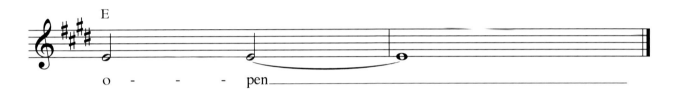

2. This is my trunk I'm a tall, tall tree
    In the summer the breezes blow through me
 I bend, I bend

3. This is my trunk I'm a tall, tall tree
    In the autumn the apples fall from me
 They drop! They drop!

4. This is my trunk I'm a tall, tall tree
    In the winter the snowflakes fall on me
 Thay fall, They fall

This is a favorite for all young children. It works well to use throughout the year and lends itself easily to beautiful motions. The trunk of the tree is the body, start at the feet and run hands up the body then bringing the arms up to become the branches that bend slowly in the wind, grow apples, receive snowflakes and slowly open beautiful blossoms. Let the motions be slow and beautiful!
The children love this song throughout the year. It's also a very good bending over exercise for all of us!

Track 2

In the Springtime

Clifford Monks

In the spring-time bun-ny rab-bits go hop hop! In the sun-shine

lit-tle bir-dies go chirp chirp! Dai-sies nod to daf-fo dils

Lit-tle chil-dren run up hills and fall down in the spring-time!

Copyright 2008 naturally you can sing™
All Rights Reserved

The Heart of a Seed

Spring Rain

Track 5 — M. T. Schunemann

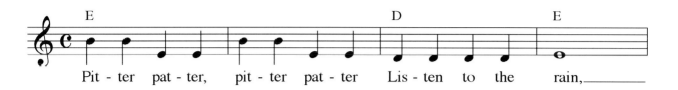

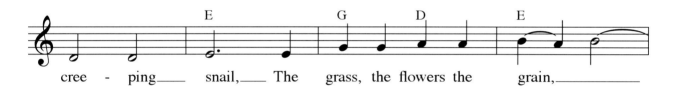

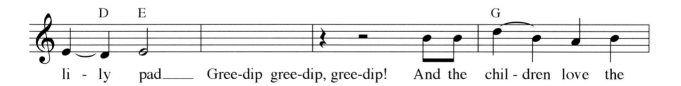
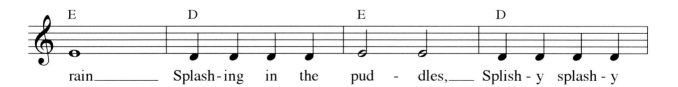

Copyright 2008 naturally you can sing™
All Rights Reserved

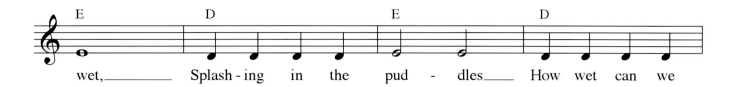
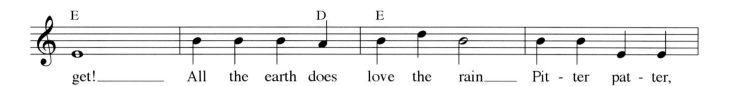

Track 6

Growing Song

Unknown
M.T.Schunemann

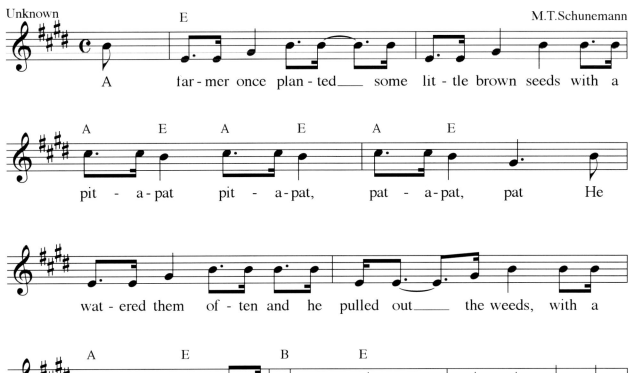

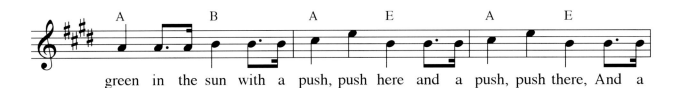

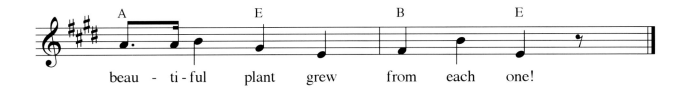

Copyright 2008 naturally you can sing™
All Rights Reserved

The Morning Star

Track 7

Chippewa

When it is dawn the sky is a-light, as the mor-ning star greets day with her light
When the sun ris-es the day it is born And show-ers its light on this spring-time morn

Drum Beat

This song is part of a special ceremony which takes place in early spring at dawn. Its purpose is to pray to the power of the far off Morning Star (Venus) to ensure that new plantings will grow into a good crop.

Pussy Willows

Track 8

Pentatonic
Chr. Morgenstern

M. T. Schunemann

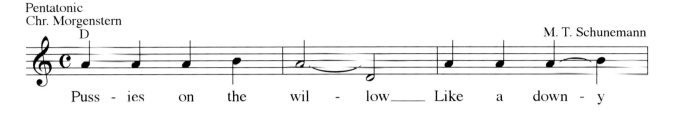
Puss - ies on the wil - low___ Like a down - y

pil - low___ Let your sil - ken grey___

Ti - ckle on my face___ Lit - tle kit - tens hid - ing,___

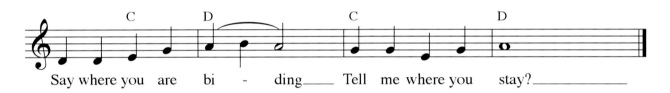
Say where you are bi - ding___ Tell me where you stay?___

Children's Lyre: Strumming

Copyright 2008 naturally you can sing™
All Rights Reserved

Caterpillar

Track 9

Pentatonic Anon.
M. T. Schunemann

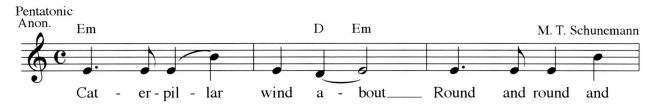
Cat - er - pil - lar wind a - bout___ Round and round and

in and out And when you're fed you spin your bed___ then go___

to___ sleep___ Deep,___ deep,___ sleep___ Then as___ a cat - er - pil - lar

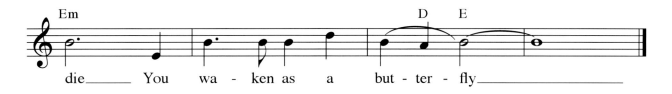
die___ You wa - ken as a but - ter - fly___

Butterflies

Over in the Meadow

Track 14

Appalachian Folk Song

O-ver in the mea-dow in the sand,— in the sun,— Lives a dear mo-ther toad and her lit-tle toa-dy one.— Hop! says the mo-ther, I hop! says the one.— So they hop and they hop in the sand,— in the sun.—

2. Over in the meadow where the stream runs so blue
   Lives a dear mother fish and her little fishes two
   Swim, says the mother, we swim, say the two
   So they swim and they swim where the stream runs so blue

3. Over in the meadow in the big oak tree
   Lives a dear mother robin and her little robins three
   Fly, says the mother, we fly, say the three
   So they fly, and they fly, round the big, oak tree

4. Over in the meadow in the reeds by the shore
   Lives a mother water rat, and her little ratties four
   Dive, says the mother, we dive, say the four
   So they dive, and they dive in the reeds by the shore

5. Over in the meadow in a sunny beehive,
   Lives a mother honey bee and her little bees five
   Buzz, says the mother, we buzz, say the five
   So they buzz, and they buzz in the sunny beehive

6, Over in the meadow in a nest built of sticks
   Lives a dear mother crow and her little crows six
   Caw, says the mother, we caw, say the six
   So they caw and they caw in their nest built of sticks

7. Over in the meadow where the grass is so even
   Lives a dear mother cricket and her little crickets seven
   Chirp, says the mother, we chirp, say the seven
   So they chirp and they chirp where the grass is so even

Nimble Fishes

Track 15
Pentatonic

M.T. Schunemann

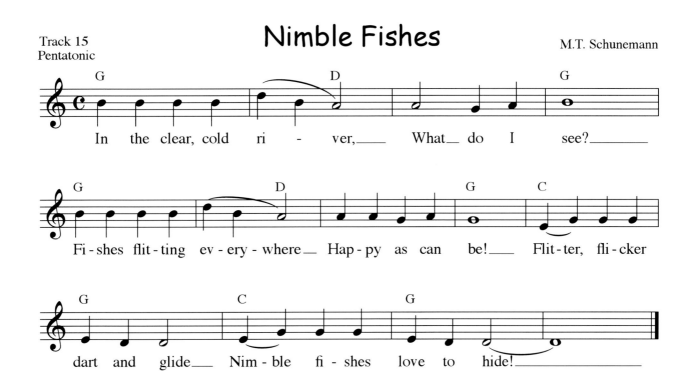

In the clear, cold ri - ver,___ What_ do I see?___
Fi - shes flit - ting ev - ery - where_ Hap - py as can be!__ Flit - ter, fli - cker
dart and glide__ Nim - ble fi - shes love to hide!___

Copyright 2008 naturally you can sing™
All Rights Reserved

Zoom! Zoom! Zoom!

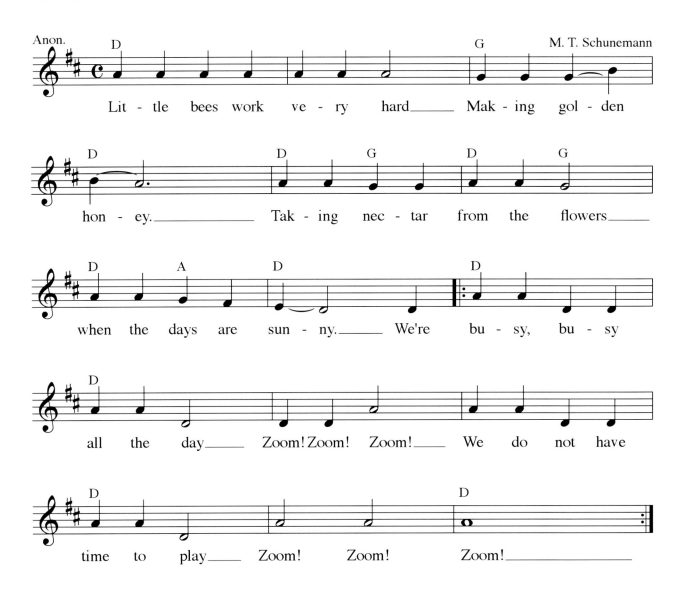

Then what do you suppose?
  A bee landed on my nose!
He said I beg your pardon,
  I thought you were a garden!

Fireflies

M. T. Schunemann

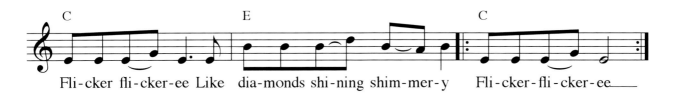

Falling Stars

Track 21
Pentatonic
M. T. Schunemann

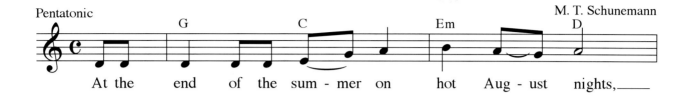
At the end of the sum-mer on hot Aug-ust nights,___

Mi-cha-el sends fall-ing stars, Bring-ing strength and light.___

In the late night hours you fall,___ Show-er-ing your star-light on all,___

Fall-ing stars,___ fall-ing stars,___ Shoot a-cross the sky,___

Fall-ing stars,___ fall-ing stars,___ Bring to earth your light!___
Bring to earth your might!___

27

Copyright 2008 naturally you can sing™
All Rights Reserved

Summer Goodbye

Track 22

Traditional German

Sum-mer good-bye,— Sum-mer good-bye,— You may no long-er— stay,

Au-tumn is on its— way, Sum-mer good-bye,— Sum-mer good-bye!—

September Passing By

Track 23

Pentatonic Anon.

M T Schunamann

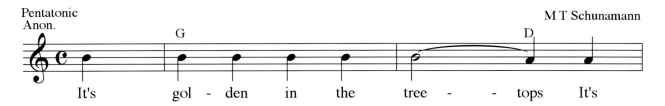
It's gol - den in the tree - - tops It's

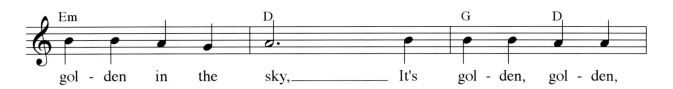
gol - den in the sky,_____ It's gol - den, gol - den,

gol - den Sep - tem - ber pass - ing by_____

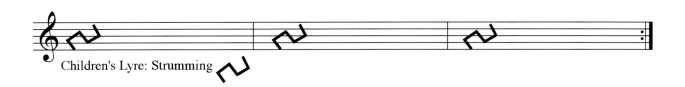
Children's Lyre: Strumming

Five Golden Leaves

Track 24
Traditional

Five gol-den leaves hang-ing from a tree, Danc-ing

gol-den in the sun,_____ Then a-long came the wind and he

blew through the town_____ Whooosh! One lit-tle leaf tumb-led

down to the ground!_____

Four golden leaves hanging from a tree
    Dancing golden in the sun
Then along came the wind and he blew through the town
    Whoosh! ...and another little leaf tumbled down to the ground!

Three golden leaves...
    Two golden leaves...
        One golden leaf...
            ...and the last little leaf tumbled down to the ground!

Copyright 2008 naturally you can sing™
All Rights Reserved

The Leaves are Green

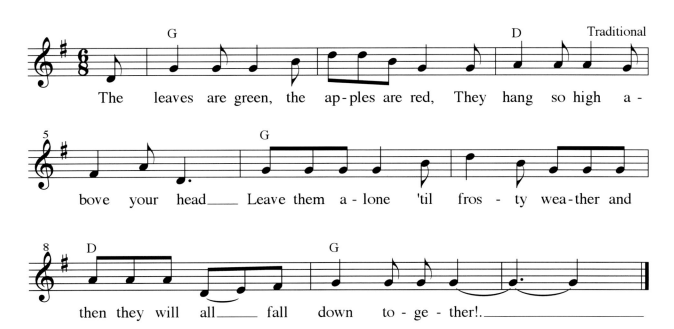

2. The leaves are green and the nuts are brown
   They hang so high and will not come down
   Leave them alone 'til frosty weather
   And then they will all come down together!

Scarlet and Yellow, Golden and Brown

Oh, Great Spirit

Track 27

Pentatonic   Native American

1) Em   Bm   2) Em   G

Oh, Great Spi - rit, Earth, Wind, Sky and Sea

3) Em   4) C   D   Em

You are in - side, and all a - round me

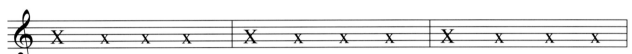

Drum Beat

* This song can also work really well as a round when children are a bit older

The Farmer

Track 28

Anon
M T Schunemann

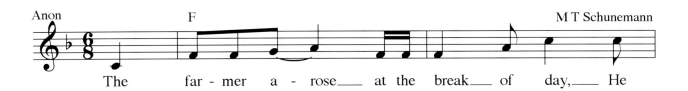
The far-mer a-rose at the break of day, He

got on his horse and he gal-loped a-way, He gal-loped a-way, He

gal-loped a-way, He got on his horse and he gal-loped a-way. Oh,

come all my men, Oh, come said he, our car-rots and tur-nips

for to see In the warm, brown earth they have grown so big

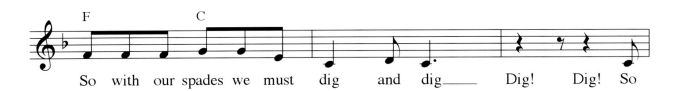
So with our spades we must dig and dig Dig! Dig! So

fetch your spades and come a-long, to dig up the roots with your

Copyright 2008 naturally you can sing™
All Rights Reserved

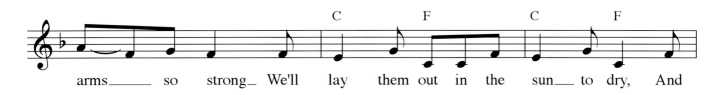
arms___ so strong_ We'll lay them out in the sun__ to dry, And

then in the cart pile them up___ so high!___

The Winds

Track 29

Pentatonic
Anon

M T Schunemann

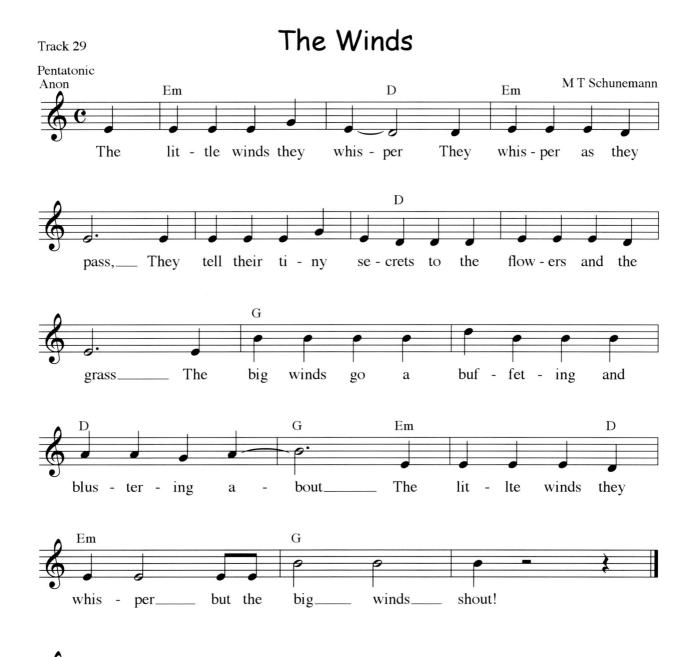

The lit-tle winds they whis-per They whis-per as they pass,___ They tell their ti-ny se-crets to the flow-ers and the grass___ The big winds go a buf-fet-ing and blus-ter-ing a-bout___ The lit-lte winds they whis-per___ but the big___ winds___ shout!

Children's Lyre

Copyright 2006 naturally you can sing™
All Rights Reserved

Jack-O-Lantern

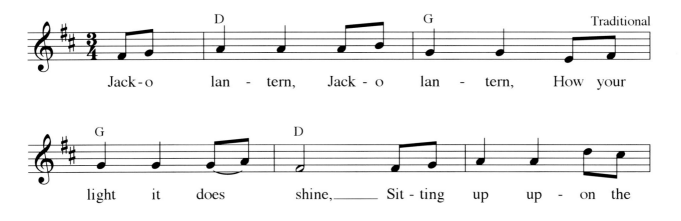

Jack-o lantern, Jack-o lantern, How your light it does shine,___ Sitting up upon the window and your light it does shine.___

2. You were once an orange pumpkin
   Sitting on a pumpkin vine
   Now you are my Jack-o-Lantern
   And your light it is mine...

Reaping Song

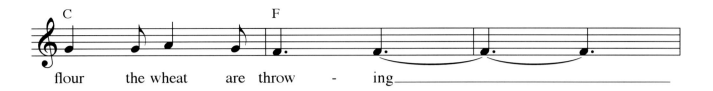

flour the wheat are throw - ing

Tossed high in air   Gol - den grain all a - round is

blow - ing   Chsshh,   Chssshh,   Chsshh

Track 33

The Apple Tree

Traditional M T Schunemann

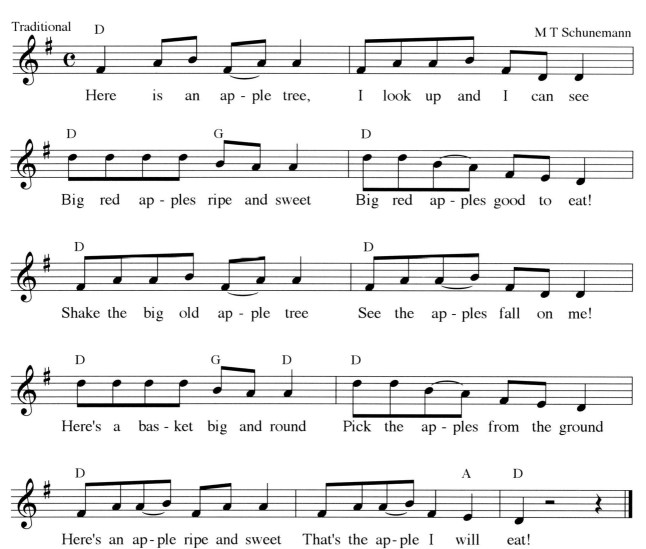

Here is an apple tree, I look up and I can see
Big red apples ripe and sweet Big red apples good to eat!
Shake the big old apple tree See the apples fall on me!
Here's a basket big and round Pick the apples from the ground
Here's an apple ripe and sweet That's the apple I will eat!

Track 34

Autumn Goodbye

Traditional German

Autumn good-bye, Autumn good-bye, You may no longer stay,
Winter is on its way, Autumn good-bye, Autumn good-bye

My Little Lamp

Track 36

Pentatonic
Anon.

M.T.Schunemann

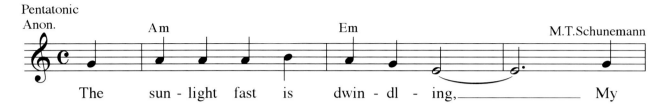
The sun-light fast is dwin-dl-ing, My

lit-tle lamp needs kin-dl-ing, Let your beams shine far, In-

to the dark night, Lit-tle lan-tern guard me

with your pre-cious light.

Children's Lyre

The North Wind Doth Blow

2. The North Wind doth blow, and we shall have snow
   And what will the swallow do then, poor thing?
   Oh do you not know that he's gone long ago
   To a country much warmer than ours, Ah!

3. The North Wind doth blow, and we shall have snow
   And what will the dormouse do then, poor thing?
   He's rolled up in a ball in his nest, oh so small,
   He'll sleep 'til it's springtime again, Ah!

Jack Frost

Track 38

Pentatonic
Anon.

M.T.Schunemann

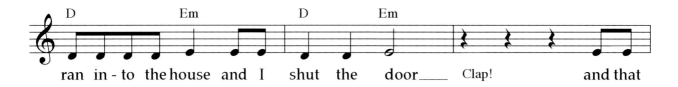

Old Man Winter

Winter Song

J. John .M.T.Schunemann

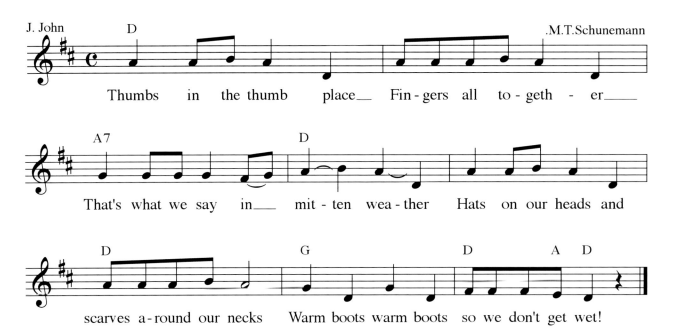

Thumbs in the thumb place— Fin-gers all to-geth-er—
That's what we say in— mit-ten wea-ther Hats on our heads and
scarves a-round our necks Warm boots warm boots so we don't get wet!

I'm a Little Snowman

Track 41

Traditional

I'm a lit-tle snow-man short and fat,___ Here is my broom-stick,

here is my hat!___ When the sun comes out I melt a-way___

Down,___ down,___ down,___ down,___ Whooops! I'm a puddle!

Mark Your Steps

Track 42

Pentatonic Anon.
M.T.Schunemann

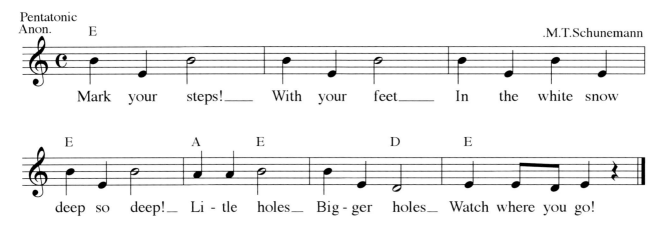

Mark your steps!__ With your feet__ In the white snow deep so deep!__ Li-tle holes__ Big-ger holes__ Watch where you go!

Oh, Where Do You Come From?

Track 43

Traditional German

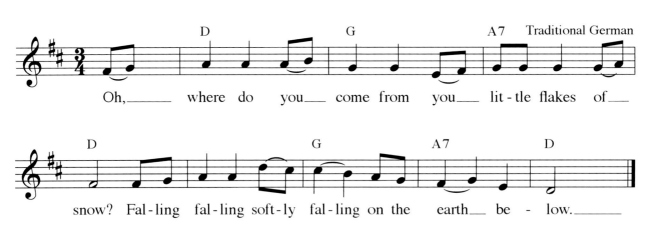

Oh,__ where do you__ come from you__ lit-tle flakes of__ snow? Fal-ling fal-ling soft-ly fal-ling on the earth__ be-low.__

2. On the trees and on the bushes, on the mountains afar
   Tell me snowflakes do you come from where the angels are?

One Star Shone

Track 44

M. T. Schunemann

I looked up care-ful-ly in-to the deep night sky, A thou-sand stars were twink-ling from on high, And one star shone so ve-ry, ve-ry bright, Up-on the dark Earth wait-ing, wait-ing for it's light.

Children's Lyre

2. The angels filled the sky with light
    And sing to the Child who is born upon this night
  And one star shone so very, very bright
    Upon the people waiting, waiting for its light

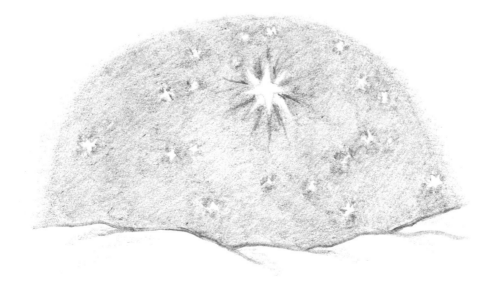

Copyright 2008 naturally you can sing™
All Rights Reserved

The Buffalo in Winter

Track 45
M.T.Schunemann

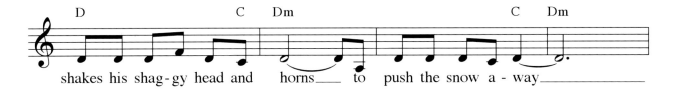

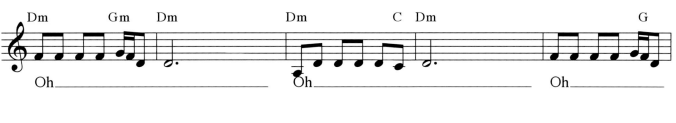

The Groundhog

Track 47
C. Aldinger

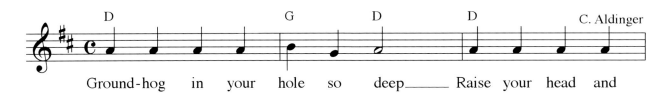
Ground-hog in your hole so deep___ Raise your head and

take a peep___ If your sha-dow makes you leap!

Curl back up and go to sleep.___

Winter Goodbye

Track 48
Traditional German

Win-ter good-bye,___ Win-ter good-bye___ You may no lon-ger___ stay,

Spring-time is on its___ way; Win-ter good-bye,___ Win-ter good-bye___

NOTES

Loving Thanks

Special thanks to the Rudolf Steiner Foundation and
the Future Values Fund for helping to make this project possible.

To my wonderful husband Sven,
who provides me with continual support, creativity, humor
and encouragement.

To our beautiful daughters Aurora and Allegra
for their joy of life and love of song.

To my dear friend Cynthia for awakening me to the wonders of nature.

To the angels who lovingly inspire and protect us all.

To the Great Spirit of God,
Creator of this incredibly beautiful earth
Which Sustains and Nourishes us all.

Let us be ever grateful and generous in sharing the Earth's bounty
and in protecting its health…
…for we are the keepers of the Earth!…

You are singing turtle dove
On the branches of the silk cotton tree
And there also is the cuckoo
And many other little birds
All are rejoicing
The songbirds of our God, our Lord…
And our Goddess has her little birds,
The turtledove, the redbird
The black and yellow songbirds and the hummingbird
These are the birds
Of the beautiful Goddess, our Lady…
If there is such happiness among the creatures
Why do our hearts not also rejoice?
At daybreak all is jubilant!
Let only joy, on songs
Enter our thoughts!
…Song of Dzitbalche

Naturally You Can Sing On Line music is available from many popular music online services.

We have included these QR codes for your convenience to be able quickally access your preferred music streaming service.

Apple Music QR code

Spotify QR code

Amazon Music QR code

Youtube QR code

Audio reference music to Naturally You can Sing Song Books is only available from your prefered online music service.